Great River Regional Library
January 2011

D0891710

New Careers for the 21st Century: Finding Your Role in the Global Renewal

GREEN CONSTRUCTION:

CREATING ENERGY-EFFICIENT, LOW-IMPACT BUILDINGS

New Careers for the 21st Century: Finding Your Role in the Global Renewal

New Careers for the
21st Century:
Finding Your Role in
the Global Renewal

GREEN CONSTRUCTION:

CREATING ENERGY-EFFICIENT, LOW-IMPACT BUILDINGS

by Malinda Miller

Mason Crest Publishers

GREEN CONSTRUCTION:

CREATING ENERGY-EFFICIENT, LOW-IMPACT BUILDINGS

Copyright © 2011 by Mason Crest Publishers. All rights reserved. No part of this publication may be reproduced or transmitted in any form or by any means, electronic or mechanical, including photocopying, recording, taping, or any information storage and retrieval system, without permission from the publisher.

MASON CREST PUBLISHERS INC.
370 Reed Road
Broomall, Pennsylvania 19008
(866)MCP-BOOK (toll free)
www.masoncrest.com

First Printing
9 8 7 6 5 4 3 2 1

Library of Congress Cataloging-in-Publication Data

Miller, Malinda, 1979–
  Green construction : creating energy-efficient, low-impact buildings / by Malinda Miller. — 1st ed.
        p. cm. — (New careers for the 21st century: finding your role in America's renewal)
  Includes bibliographical references and index.
  ISBN 978-1-4222-1815-0   ISBN 978-1-4222-1811-2 (series)
  ISBN 978-1-4222-2036-8 (ppb)   ISBN 978-1-4222-2032-0 (series ppb)
  1. Sustainable construction. I. Title.
  TH880.M55 2010
  690'.2—dc22
                              2010010013

Produced by Harding House Publishing Service, Inc.
www.hardinghousepages.com
Interior design by MK Bassett-Harvey.
Cover design by Torque Advertising + Design.
Printed in USA by Bang Printing.

CONTENTS

INTRODUCTION

Be careful as you begin to plan your career.

To get yourself in the best position to begin the career of your dreams, you need to know what the "green world" will look like and what jobs will be created and what jobs will become obsolete. Just think, according to the Bureau of Labor Statistics, the following jobs are expected to severely decline by 2012:

- word processors and data-entry keyers

- stock clerks and order fillers

- secretaries

- electrical and electronic equipment assemblers

- computer operators

- telephone operators

- postal service mail sorters and processing-machine operators

- travel agents

These are just a few of the positions that will decrease or become obsolete as we move forward into the century.

You need to know what the future jobs will be. How do you find them? One way is to look where money is being invested. Many firms and corporations are now making investments in startup and research enterprises. These companies may become the "Microsoft" and "Apple" of the twenty-first century. Look at what is being researched and what technology is needed to obtain the results.

Green world, green economy, green technology—they all say the same things: the way we do business today is changing. Every industry will be shaped by the world's new focus on creating a sustainable lifestyle, one that won't deplete our natural and economic resources.

The possibilities are unlimited. Almost any area that will conserve energy and reduce the dependency on fossil fuels is open to new and exciting career paths. Many of these positions have not even been identified yet and will only come to light as the technology progresses and new discoveries are made in the way we use that technology. And the best part about this is that our government is behind us. The U.S. government wants to help you get the education and training you'll need to succeed and grow in this new and changing economy. The U.S. Department of Labor has launched a series of initiatives to support and promote green job creation. To view the report, visit: www.dol.gov/dol/green/earthday_reportA.pdf.

The time to decide on your future is now. This series, NEW CAREERS FOR THE 21ST CENTURY: FINDING YOUR ROLE IN THE GLOBAL RENEWAL, can act as the first step toward your continued education, training, and career path decisions. Take the first steps that will lead you—and the planet—to a productive and sustainable future.

Mike Puglisi
Department of Labor, District I Director (New York/New Jersey)
IAWP (International Association of Workforce Professionals)

Organic buildings are the strength and lightness of the spiders' spinning, buildings qualified by light, bred by native character to environment, married to the ground.

—Frank Lloyd Wright

ABOUT THE QUOTE

Not every building that's made is as beautiful as those designed by Frank Lloyd Wright—but construction is always a creative act, making something new that didn't exist before. And there's an even greater sense of satisfaction in building in way that is in harmony with the environment.

CHAPTER **1**
WHAT IS CONSTRUCTION?

WORDS TO KNOW

Infrastructure: The roads, utility services, and public institutions that supply the basic needs of the country.

Civil engineering: The branch of engineering that designs and maintains public structures, such as roads, bridges, and dams.

Prefabrication: The production of parts ahead of time to allow for quick assembly and installation on site.

Recession: A period of economic decline, when there is less money and fewer jobs.

Many books, movies and television shows have predicted the world will look very different in the future. Humans will live in space. We will travel via rocket ship or personal flying vehicles. Robots will live among us, or even challenge humans for control of the Earth. So, what does the twenty-first century actually hold for us? How will our lives change?

Though we can look forward to as-yet-unknown advances in science and technology, our lives in the future will probably not be drastically different from our lives now. In fact, we can already see the future developing all around us, from the increasing number of hybrid vehicles on our highways to the mp3 players in our hands. These developments will have lasting impacts on the world and on workers of the future, because with a new world comes new career opportunities.

The young adults of today will be the job force of tomorrow, so choosing a career that will best fit with the needs of the changing world will be important to job satisfaction and a successful life. With the vast array of career and job options, it will also be important for young adults to understand which work will be the best match for their interests, talents, goals, and personality types.

Certain job industries are expected to gain importance within the early decades of the twenty-first century. Construction is one of the industries that will probably grow at a faster than average rate. According to the United States Bureau of Labor Statistics, the number of jobs across all industries is expected to increase by 11 percent through the year 2018, while jobs in the construction industry are expected grow by 19 percent.

What Is Construction?

Construction workers build houses, apartments, factories, offices, schools, roads, and bridges, and install utilities. Construction activities include the building of new structures as well as additions, repairs, or other modifications to existing ones.

Preparation of sites for new construction and subdivision of land for sale as building sites also are included in the construction sector.

Construction businesses usually manage construction activities at many project sites. Work is obtained through prime contracts (contracts with the owners of construction projects) or through subcontracts (contracts with other construction businesses).

CONSTRUCTION EMPLOYMENT COMPOSITION BY AGE

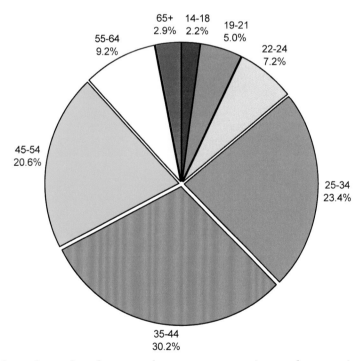

This chart shows that there may be many construction workers nearing retirement in the next decade. These job openings will create new job opportunities for young workers.

Construction Industry

The construction industry is divided into three major segments: the construction of buildings, heavy and *civil engineering* construction, and specialty trade contractors.

Construction of Buildings

The construction of buildings segment includes contractors, usually called general contractors, who build residential (houses and apartment buildings), industrial (factories), commercial (office buildings), and other buildings. General contractors take responsibility for the complete job. Although general contractors may do

Construction of buildings may include new building, additions or alterations to existing structures, maintenance, and repairs.

Construction Trade Jobs

- boilermakers
- brickmasons, blockmasons, and stonemasons
- carpenters
- carpet, floor, and tile installers and finishers
- cement masons, concrete finishers, segmental pavers, and terrazzo workers
- construction and building inspectors
- construction equipment operators
- construction laborers
- drywall and ceiling tile installers, tapers, plasterers, and stucco masons
- electricians
- elevator installers and repairers
- glaziers
- hazardous materials removal workers
- insulation workers
- painters and paperhangers
- plumbers, pipelayers, pipefitters, and steamfitters
- roofers
- sheet metal workers
- structural and reinforcing iron and metal workers

a portion of the work with their own crews, they often subcontract most of the work to heavy construction or specialty trade contractors.

HEAVY AND CIVIL ENGINEERING CONSTRUCTION

Heavy and civil engineering construction contractors build sewers, roads, highways, bridges, tunnels, and other projects related to the country's *infrastructure*. Specialty trade contractors also work on these projects. Specialty trade contractors in heavy and civil engineering construction are usually performing activities that are specific to heavy and civil engineering construction projects and are not normally needed in building construction.

SPECIALTY TRADE CONTRACTORS

Specialty trade contractors perform specialized activities related to all types of construction, such as carpentry, pouring concrete, site preparation, painting, plumbing, and electrical work. Specialty trade contractors usually do the work of only one trade, such as painting, carpentry, or electrical work, or of two or more closely related trades, such as plumbing and heating. Beyond adapting their work to each project

Did You Know?
Construction is the second-largest industry in the United States, employing about 7 million workers.

and working alongside other trades, specialty trade contractors have no responsibility for the structure as a whole. They obtain orders for their work from general contractors, architects, or property owners. Repair work is almost always done on direct order

Jobs for bricklayers—including brickmasons, blockmasons, and stonemasons—are expected to increase by 12 percent through 2018.

What Kind of Person Are You?

Career-counseling experts know that certain kinds of people do best in certain kinds of jobs. John L. Holland developed the following list of personality types and the kinds of jobs that are the best match for each type. See which one (or two) are most like you. The more you understand yourself, the better you'll be able to make a good career plan for yourself.

- **Realistic personality:** This kind of person likes to do practical, hands-on work. He or she will most enjoy working with materials that can be touched and manipulated, such as wood, steel, tools, and machinery. This personality type enjoys jobs that require working outdoors, but he or she does NOT enjoy jobs that require a lot of paperwork or close teamwork with others.

- **Investigative personality:** This personality type likes to work with ideas. He or she will enjoy jobs that require lots of thinking and researching. Jobs that require mental problem solving will be a good fit for this personality.

- **Artistic personality:** This type of person enjoys working with forms, designs, and patterns. She or he likes jobs that require self-expression—and that don't require following a definite set of rules.

- **Social personality:** Jobs that require lots of teamwork with others, as well as teaching others, are a good match for this personality type. These jobs often involve helping others in some way.

- **Enterprising personality:** This person will enjoy planning and starting new projects, even if that involves a degree of risk-taking. He or she is good at making decisions and leading others.

- **Conventional personality:** An individual with this type of personality likes to follow a clear set of procedures or routines. He or she doesn't want to be the boss but prefers to work under someone else's leadership. Jobs that require working with details and facts (more than ideas) are a good fit for this personality.

from owners, occupants, architects, or rental agents. Specialty trade contractors perform most of their work at the construction site, although they may have shops where they perform *prefabrication* and other work.

RECENT DEVELOPMENTS IN CONSTRUCTION

The construction industry was strongly affected by the credit crisis and *recession* that began in December 2007. Housing prices fell and foreclosures of homes rose sharply, particularly in overbuilt areas of the country. New housing construction, while still ongoing, dropped significantly. The recession is expected to impact other types of construction as well. Retailers are not building many new stores, and state and local governments are reducing spending. However, as energy costs have risen, some companies are finding it necessary to build or renovate buildings that are not energy efficient. Green construction is an area that is increasingly popular and involves making buildings as environmentally friendly and energy efficient as possible by using more recyclable and earth-friendly products.

*What's the use
of a fine house if
you haven't got a
tolerable planet to
put it on?*

—Henry David Thoreau

ABOUT THE QUOTE

Green construction is a new way of looking at the building industry, one that creates buildings while protecting the planet.

CHAPTER 2
GREEN CONSTRUCTION

WORDS TO KNOW

Sustainable: Able to be maintained, especially by keeping a balance with the environment and avoiding using up natural resources.

Greenhouse gases: Gases, such as carbon dioxide, methane, and chlorofluorocarbons, that absorb heat and trap it in the atmosphere, contribute to climate change.

Renewable energy: Energy obtained from sources other than fossil fuels, such as solar power, wind power, hydropower, and geothermic power.

Accreditation: Official authorization given after certain standards are met.

Building green does not mean constructing houses or office buildings that are green in color! Green construction is high-performance building or *sustainable* building, and it refers to the practice of creating structures and using processes that are environmentally responsible and that use resources efficiently throughout a building's life-cycle, from the building site to its design, from construction, operation, and maintenance through renovation and even deconstruction (tearing it down). This practice expands and complements the classical building design concerns of cost, usefulness, durability, and comfort.

WHY BUILD GREEN?

Humans have changed the world. Emissions from our homes and cars, our offices and airplanes—our modern way of life—have led to a global climate crisis. According to NOAA and NASA data, the Earth's average surface temperature has increased by about 1.2 to 1.4° F (.7 to .8° C) in the last 100 years. The increase in carbon dioxide ($CO2$) and other *greenhouse gases* from cars,

IMPACTS OF CONSTRUCTION

ASPECTS OF BUILT ENVIRONMENT	CONSUMPTION	ENVIRONMENTAL EFFECTS	ULTIMATE EFFECTS
siting design construction operation maintenance renovation deconstruction	energy water materials natural resources	waste air pollution water pollution indoor pollution heat islands storm-water runoff noise	harm to human health environment degradation loss of resources

All segments of the construction industry can potentially impact the environment. Green construction planning needs to begin with the first phase of a project in order to reduce impacts across all levels.

the use of electricity, the raising of livestock, and other human activities are the likely cause of this warming trend. Scientists studying climate change predict that if the warming continues at this rate, there will be drastic negative effects on the environment and on our lives.

Did You Know?
The eight warmest years on record (since 1850) have all occurred since 1998, with the warmest year being 2005.

Houses, office buildings, and other establishments emit a high level of greenhouse gases because they use a large amount of energy for heating, cooling, lighting, and operating appliances and equipment. According to the United States Environmental Protection Agency (EPA), in the United States, buildings account for:

• 39 percent of total energy use.

• 12 percent of the total water consumption.

• 68 percent of total electricity consumption.

• 38 percent of the carbon dioxide emissions.

Green building strategies help reduce these emissions and thus reduce the impacts buildings have on the environment. Green construction methods can be used at any stage of building, from design and construction to renovation and deconstruction. However, the most significant benefits are obtained if green building methods are a part of the project from the earliest stages of planning.

WHAT MAKES CONSTRUCTION GREEN?

PLANNING AND SITE SELECTION

Though a construction project can be "greened" at any step in the building process, the most effective green construction begins with at the earliest stages—the design and planning phases. In addition to standard building issues, the planning phases of green construction must consider landscape impact of site selection, pollution prevention, selection of sustainable materials, health impacts, and energy consumption. The right design plan will lead to a completed building with the smallest environmental impact.

ENERGY AND WATER EFFICIENCY

The main goal of most green construction projects is to minimize energy consumption. This can be accomplished through the use of **renewable energy** sources, efficient insulation, window selection and placement, roofing material, and building orientation and site selection.

Reducing water usage is also a vital consideration in green building. To prevent contributing to the overuse of water supplies, green contractors will design buildings to use less water but also to purify and re-use wastewater. Buildings may also feature landscaping that reduces water usage (for example, by using native plants that survive without extra watering).

Did You Know?
If every household in the United States replaced standard light bulbs with ENERGY STAR® bulbs, we would prevent greenhouse gases equivalent to the emissions from nearly 10 million cars.

Potential Benefits of Green Building

Environmental Benefits
- enhance and protect biodiversity and ecosystems
- improve air and water quality
- reduce waste streams
- conserve and restore natural resources

Economic Benefits
- reduce operating costs
- create, expand, and shape markets for green product and services
- improve occupant productivity
- optimize life-cycle economic performance

Social Benefits
- enhance occupant comfort and health
- heighten aesthetic qualities
- minimize strain on local infrastructure
- improve overall quality of life

SUSTAINABLE MATERIALS

Green building materials are nontoxic, reused, recycled, or made from renewable resources. Renewable resources are those natural materials that can be replaced faster than they are consumed by human usage. For example, bamboo is considered a renewable resource, because unlike trees, bamboo can be regrown to maturity within a few years. Whenever possible, locally sourced materials should be used to minimize the energy and emissions from transporting materials.

POLLUTION AND WASTE REDUCTION

Green buildings aim to create healthy indoor environments with minimal pollutants by improving indoor air quality. Building with low or zero-emissions materials improves air quality, as does providing proper ventilation.

Did You Know?
Americans use an average of 100 gallons of water each day per person—enough to fill 1,600 drinking glasses.

Construction usually creates a large amount of waste. In fact, materials generated during construction and demolition (C&D) account for almost 40 percent of the country's total solid waste. Reducing and recycling these C&D materials conserves landfill space, reduces the environmental impact of producing new materials, creates jobs, and can reduce overall building project expenses. Industrial waste products can also be recycled for use as materials in the construction industry.

Did You Know?
Bamboo can grow up to
three feet a day!

The use of sustainable materials, such as bamboo flooring, in building construction is one way to make a construction project greener.

Green building plans should also design environmentally responsible methods for processing the solid waste that will be generated once the building is in use.

How Can You Get Involved in Green Building?

For the most part, the education and training required for work on green construction projects will be the same as the education and training required for standard construction projects. Construction workers (usually the contractors) can take courses and exams to earn professional green *accreditation* through the Leadership in Energy and Environmental Design (LEED) certification program. Certification indicates that the worker is dedicated to green building and that he or she has a thorough understanding of the rating systems that will ultimately qualify a building as "green."

The EPA currently does not have a green building certification program. However, the EPA and the U.S. Department of Energy's ENERGY STAR program addresses one of the most important aspects of green building: energy. ENERGY STAR qualifies new or renovated buildings as energy efficient, and it awards the ENERGY STAR label.

A variety of private and nonprofit green building certification programs exist in the marketplace, including LEED and Green Globes. The Public-Private Partnership for Advancing Housing Technology maintains a list of national and state Green Building Certification Programs for housing at www.pathnet.org/sp.asp?id=20978.

If You Have a Realistic Personality . . .

Here are some of the best jobs for you within the green construction industry. (These tables also include the average salary you can expect to earn in U.S. dollars in these jobs and how many openings are projected to exist in the United States each year for these jobs. The information comes from the U.S. Bureau of Labor Statistics.)

JOB	ANNUAL EARNINGS	ANNUAL OPENINGS
plumbers, pipefitters, and steamfitters	$44,000	68,643
construction & building inspectors	$48,330	12,606
carpenters	$37,660	223,225
electricians	$44,780	79,083
roofers	$33,240	38,398
general construction laborer	$27,310	257,407
heating & air conditioning installers	$38,160	27,100
installation, maintenance, & repair workers	$38,360	29,719
architects & civil drafters	$43,310	16,238
hazardous materials removal workers	$36,330	1,933
refuse & recyclable collectors	$29,420	37,785
welders, cutters, solderers, & brazers	$32,270	61,125
structural iron & steel workers	$42,130	6,969
insulation workers	$36,570	5,787
pipelayers	$31,280	8,902

We won't have
a society if we
destroy the
environment.
—Margaret Mead

ABOUT THE QUOTE

The world has realized that we can no longer live as though human society and the natural world were two separate things. We are connected to
the planet, and our health depends on protecting it. Green construction
recognizes this reality.

CHAPTER 3
EDUCATION AND TRAINING

WORDS TO KNOW

Apprentice: A person who works under a skilled employer (journeyman) to learn a trade while working and earning wages.

Vocational: Having to do with education that is focused on a certain occupation and its skills.

Baccalaureate degree: The degree given to a student who completes four years of undergraduate studies; also known as a bachelor's degree.

Associate degree: The degree given to a student who completes two years of study, usually given by community colleges.

Workers in the construction industry have a variety of educational and training backgrounds. A worker beginning right out of high school usually starts as a laborer, a helper, or an *apprentice*. While some laborers and helpers can learn their jobs in a few days, the more skilled jobs require years to learn and are usually learned through a combination of classroom instruction and on-the-job training.

TRADES WORKERS

Construction trades workers and specialized trades workers such as carpenters, bricklayers, plumbers, heating, air-conditioning, and refrigeration mechanics and installers most often get their formal instruction by attending a local technical or trade school, participating in an apprenticeship, or taking part in an employer-provided training program. In addition, they learn their craft by working with more experienced workers.

Safety training is required for most jobs, since construction is one of the most dangerous occupations based on the number of on-the-job injuries.

English language skills are essential for workers to advance within their trade. Other language skills may also be beneficial (for example Spanish language skills can be useful in attaining supervisory positions, since many construction workers are Spanish speakers).

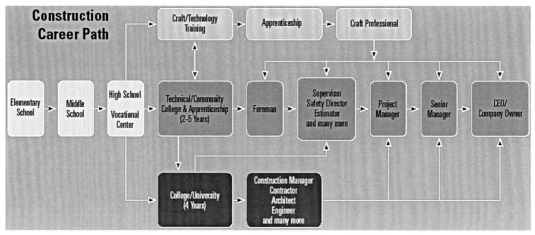

There are multiple routes to a career in construction. All of these, however, involve finishing high school or vocational training.

Interested in an Apprenticeship?

While you are in still in school, there are steps you can take to better prepare yourself.

1. Learn basic math skills, an important part of the building construction trades. You'll need basic math to know where to cut, how much material is needed, and how things will fit together.

2. Study basic English reading and writing to make learning a trade and communicating on the job easier.

3. If shop classes are available in your school, take what's offered or ask your school to develop new shop classes. Make your needs known—you have more power than you know.

4. You can also contact the various trade groups in your area and ask them if they have or can recommend any pre-apprenticeship programs. A pre-apprenticeship program is a great way to learn whether you really like a particular trade or want to choose another.

5. Volunteer for Habitat for Humanity or other opportunities without pay that allow you to try out construction.

6. If you know someone in construction, ask if you can job shadow. (This means you follow the person around while he or she works.) Some school districts have this program available.

7. Take every opportunity you can to work with your hands.

8. Look for a part-time job in a hardware store, to get exposure to the industry, tools, and supplies, and a sense of the culture of the business.

9. Search the Internet for opportunities in your area.

(From https://www.dir.ca.gov/DAS/IBuiltIt/youth-what-you-can-do.html)

Training or certification in "green," energy-efficient construction is also available and can help workers find employment in today's environmentally conscious job market.

Apprenticeships

Apprenticeships provide the most thorough training. Apprenticeships usually last between three and five years, and consist of on-the-job training and 144 hours or more of related classroom instruction each year. Instead of required hours of training, some apprenticeship programs now use competency standards, which make it possible to complete a program in a shorter time. Those who enroll in apprenticeship programs usually are at least eighteen years old and in good physical condition. Many employers or programs require applicants to pass background checks.

Technical Schools

Depending on the occupation, there may be technical or *vocational* schools that train students to perform a given occupation's tasks. Those who enter construction from technical or vocational schools also may complete apprenticeship training; technical or vocational school graduates progress at a somewhat faster pace because they already have had courses such as mathematics, mechanical drawing, and woodworking.

Community Colleges

Community colleges offer another option for students interested in a career in construction. Community colleges are good places to learn job skills for a number of reasons. They have low tuition

Real-Life Apprentice

At the close of 2003, the Alfred Zampa Memorial Bridge in Vallejo, California, began bearing nearly 36,000 people across the Carquinez Strait on their morning commute to work. Jeremiah Johnson joined the bridge project in the second phase of his ironworker apprenticeship, having completed a pre-apprenticeship program at the National Ironworkers Training Program for American Indians in Chicago. But he started out a nineteen-year old on the Navajo Reservation in Shiprock, New Mexico.

Jeremiah joined Job Corps, the country's largest and most comprehensive residential, education, and job-training program for at-risk youth, and traveled to the Kicking Horse Job Corps center in Montana, the nation's only Job Corps center for Native Americans. During his stint with Job Corps, he saw a flyer for the ironworker pre-apprenticeship program and decided to check it out.

Candidates leave home, family, and friends, and travel to Chicago, where they live off a small stipend that barely pays for meals and housing for their twelve-week course. At the end of the course, students make a work location wish list. Not everyone gets their first choice, but all are offered jobs.

California was one of Jeremiah's top-five choices. Working with the variety of journeypeople, tasks, and materials on the Zampa Bridge project broadened Jeremiah's perspective on the ironworking trade and helped him discover his strengths.

"Me being an apprentice, it's great I took the opportunity to learn these things first hand, especially with the journeymen I work with," says Jeremiah.

What he likes most about the work is waking up every morning, finding out what's new and what he can get done that day. He also likes the variety of journeypeople who mentor him, helping him find which form of ironwork he's best at and discovering the kind of person he is.

(From http://www.dir.ca.gov/Apprenticeship/ApprenticeshipStory3.htm)

and an open-admissions policy, and they offer many courses, including classes that will help prepare students for the construction industry. Community colleges are also flexible; at most community colleges, nearly 50 percent of the students work full time, so they offer courses at convenient times. Apprenticeship programs are increasingly linked to community college programs.

Many workers choose a community college when they want to enter a new field or upgrade their skills in order to advance their career. A person with a college degree often attends a community college to update work skills.

Classroom instruction is a part of many apprenticeship programs. This will be combined with hands-on training from an experienced construction worker.

LICENSING REQUIREMENTS

A few occupations have licensing requirements. Crane operators, electricians, plumbers, and heating and air-conditioning mechanics and installers are required to have a license in most states. There are often separate licenses for contractors and workers. Other occupations do not have strict licensing requirements but often have voluntary certifications. These certifications show evidence of professionalism, knowledge, and abilities to potential employers and consumers.

Certification is administered by associations related to specific trades but is offered by other organizations as well. Green building certification is available from private organizations, such as Leadership in Energy and Environmental Design (LEED). The Green Building Certification Institute (GBCI) administers LEED professional credentials. Licensing and certification requirements may include years of work experience, classroom instruction, and/or exams. Licenses and certifications need to be renewed on a regular basis; GBCI requires that any credentials awarded for passing a LEED exam need to be updated and maintained every two years by taking additional courses. This ensures that workers stay up to date with the latest developments in green construction.

CAREER ADVANCEMENT

To further develop their skills, construction trades workers can work on a variety of projects. Flexibility and a willingness to adopt new techniques, as well as the ability to get along with people, are essential for advancement. Those who are skilled in all facets of the trade and who show good leadership qualities may be promoted to supervisor or construction manager. Construction managers may advance to superintendent of larger projects or go into the business side of construction. Some go into business for themselves as contractors.

Strong communication skills are important for supervisors and contractors, as they work with clients and subcontractors. Basic Spanish language skills can be a benefit to workers who plan to rise to supervisory positions, since Spanish-speaking workers form a large portion of the construction workforce in many areas. Learning Spanish allows the supervisor to communicate safety and work instructions to these workers.

Outside the construction industry, construction trades workers may transfer to jobs such as construction building inspector, purchasing agent, sales representative for building supply companies, or technical or vocational school instructor. To advance to a management position, additional education and training are recommended.

Laborers and helpers advance in the construction trades occupations by acquiring experience and skill in various phases of the craft. As they demonstrate ability to perform tasks, they move to progressively more challenging work. As their skills broaden, they are allowed to work more independently, and responsibilities and earnings increase. They may qualify for jobs in related, more highly skilled occupations. For example, after several years of experience, painters' helpers may become skilled painters.

Managerial Positions

Managerial personnel usually have a college degree or considerable experience in their specialty. The American Council for Construction Education (ACCE) is the accrediting agency for four-year *baccalaureate degree* programs and two-year *associate degree* programs in construction, construction science, construction management, and construction technology. Individuals who enter construction with college degrees usually start as management trainees or as assistants to construction managers. Those who receive degrees in construction science often start as field engineers, schedulers, or cost estimators. College graduates may advance to positions such as assistant manager, construction manager, general superintendent, cost estimator, construction building inspector, general manager, or top executive, contractor, or consultant. Although a college education is not always required, administrative workers often hold degrees in business administration, finance, accounting, or similar fields.

Civil Engineering Jobs

A bachelor's degree in engineering is needed for almost all entry-level engineering jobs. College graduates with a degree in a science or mathematics may qualify for certain jobs. A civil engineer must get a license from his or her state to offer services directly to the public. A license requires four years of relevant work experience and completion and passing of an exam. Beginning engineers often work under an experienced engineer to get their required work experience. Civil engineers may also choose to become certified in a specific area of the industry. Though not required for work in the same way as a license, certification may help lead to state licensure, may be required for certain projects, or may give the engineer an edge over other job applicants.

SELF-EMPLOYMENT

Many construction workers start their own businesses. Construction workers may need only a moderate financial investment to become contractors, and they can run their businesses from their homes, hiring additional construction workers only

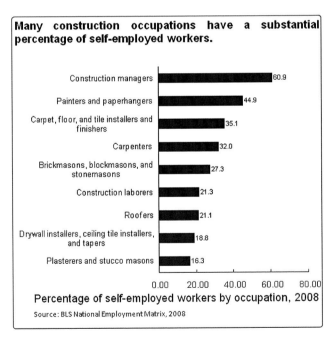

Many different types of construction workers choose to start their own businesses. As this chart shows, over 60% of construction managers or contractors are self-employed.

If You Have an Investigative Personality . . .

Here are some of the best jobs for you within the green construction industry.

JOB	ANNUAL EARNINGS	ANNUAL OPENINGS
environmental, mechanical, & industrial engineers	$75,350	29,000
mechanical engineering technicians	$47,280	3,710

If You Have a Social or Artistic Personality . . .

The construction industry may not be the best match for you. There are fewer opportunities within this industry for social contact and artistic expression than in other kinds of jobs.

as needed for specific projects. The contract construction field, however, is very competitive, and the rate of business turnover is high. Taking courses in business or earning certifications in special fields, such as green construction, helps to improve the chances for success.

We are seeing the birth of a new perspective of the world, where ecology and economics are two sides of the same coin.

—Leif Johansson

ABOUT THE QUOTE

Green construction promises to be a profitable industry in the years ahead. This means you can do your part to protect our planet—and make money in the process!

CHAPTER 4
JOB OPPORTUNITIES?

WORDS TO KNOW

Terrazzo: Flooring or countertop material that looks like marble.

Glaziers: People who cut flat glass to the right size.

Architect: A person responsible for designing and drawing detailed plans of buildings.

Natural disasters: Events, such as tornados, hurricanes, floods, or earthquakes that impact the environment and negatively affect human lives.

Benefits: Non-wage payments supplied by an employer, which supply an employee with compensations such as insurance coverage, disability protection, and retirement plans.

WORKING CONDITIONS

Construction workers need to be healthy and physically fit because the work often requires a lot of standing, bending, stooping, and lifting and carrying heavy objects.

Construction work is often potentially unsafe. According to the U.S. Bureau of Labor Statistics, construction workers experienced work-related injury and illness rates higher than the national average. To avoid injury, workers wear safety clothing, such as gloves, hardhats, and devices to protect their eyes, mouth, or hearing, as needed.

Most employees in the construction industry work full time, and many work overtime. Construction workers may work evenings, weekends, and holidays to finish a job or take care of an emergency. If bad weather halts a project, workers usually do not get paid.

Which Construction Career Is Right for You?

A student or young adult interested in a construction career has many choices for his or her career path. Knowing what you are interested in ahead of time will help you make the right choices regarding education and training. Take a look at the boxed material on personality types at the end of each chapter in this book.

If you know you enjoy physical labor and want to enter right into the job market, then college is not the right decision. On the other hand, if you are interested in engineering or in helping to design and plan buildings or heavy construction projects, be prepared for a much longer educational path. Knowing what each job does will help guide you down the best career path.

Trades Workers

Most workers in construction are construction trades workers. Trades workers are classified as structural, finishing, or mechanical workers.

Industry	Employment	Percent
Construction, total	7,214.9	100.0
Construction of buildings	1,659.3	23.0
Residential building	832.1	11.5
Nonresidential building construction	827.2	11.5
Heavy and civil engineering construction	970.3	13.4
Utility system construction	451.3	6.3
Highway, street, and bridge construction	328.9	4.6
Land subdivision	80.8	1.1
Other heavy and civil engineering construction	109.3	1.5
Specialty trade contractors	4,585.3	63.6
Building equipment contractors	2,023.1	28.0
Foundation, structure, and building exterior contractors	987.8	13.7
Building finishing contractors	912.8	12.7
Other specialty trade contractors	661.6	9.2

SOURCE: BLS National Employment Matrix, 2008-18

This table shows the distribution of employment in the construction industry. Numbers shown are in the thousands, so that the total number of jobs is about 7.2 million.

STRUCTURAL WORKERS

Structural workers build the main internal and external framework of a structure and include carpenters; construction equipment operators; brickmasons, blockmasons, and stonemasons; cement masons and concrete finishers; and structural and reinforcing iron and metal workers.

FINISHING WORKERS

Finishing workers perform the tasks that give a structure its final appearance and may include carpenters; drywall installers; ceiling tile installers; plasterers and stucco masons; segmental

Specialty trade contractors made up the largest percentage of employed workers in the construction industry in 2008. 63.6 percent of all construction jobs were in the special trade segment.

pavers; *terrazzo* workers; painters and paperhangers; *glaziers*; roofers; carpet, floor, and tile installers and finishers; and insulation workers.

MECHANICAL WORKERS

Mechanical workers install the equipment and material for basic building operations and may include pipelayers, plumbers, pipefitters, and steamfitters; electricians; sheet metal workers; and heating, air-conditioning, and refrigeration mechanics and installers.

WHAT DO TRADES WORKERS DO?

- *Boilermakers* make, install, and repair boilers, vats, and other large vessels that hold liquids and gases.

- *Brickmasons, blockmasons, and stonemasons* build and repair walls, floors, partitions, fireplaces, chimneys, and other structures with brick, pre-cast masonry panels, concrete block, stone, and other masonry materials.

- *Carpenters* construct, erect, install, or repair structures and fixtures made of wood, such as framing walls and partitions, putting in doors and windows, building stairs, laying hardwood floors, and hanging kitchen cabinets.

- *Carpet, floor, and tile installers* and *finishers* lay floor coverings, apply tile and marble, and sand and finish wood floors in a variety of buildings.

- *Cement masons, concrete finishers, segmental pavers,* and *terrazzo workers* smooth and finish poured concrete surfaces and work with concrete and other materials to create sidewalks, curbs, roadways, floors, countertops, or other surfaces.

• *Construction equipment operators,* also known as *operating engineers,* use machinery that moves construction materials, earth, and other heavy materials and applies asphalt and concrete to roads and other structures.

• *Drywall installers, ceiling installers,* and *tapers* fasten drywall panels to the inside framework of residential houses and other buildings and prepare these panels for painting by taping and finishing joints and imperfections.

• *Electricians* install, connect, test, and maintain building electrical systems, which also can include lighting, climate control, security, and communications.

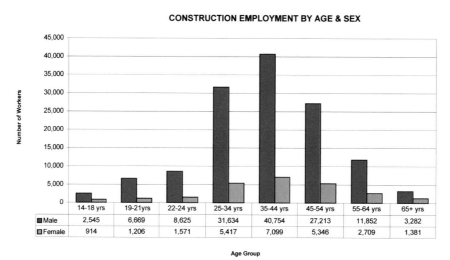

CONSTRUCTION EMPLOYMENT BY AGE & SEX

	14-18 yrs	19-21yrs	22-24 yrs	25-34 yrs	35-44 yrs	45-54 yrs	55-64 yrs	65+ yrs
Male	2,545	6,669	8,625	31,634	40,754	27,213	11,852	3,282
Female	914	1,206	1,571	5,417	7,099	5,346	2,709	1,381

Age Group

Men far outnumber women in the construction industry, but most workers (male or female) are between 25–54 years old.

Women in Construction

The stereotypical image of a construction worker is male. Women are often only pictured at a construction site as the objects of whistles and rude comments. But there are some female construction workers (though not nearly as many as there are men). In 2007, women comprised nearly half of the total workforce in the country at 46.4%, but only 9.2% of the 9.7 million construction-related jobs belonged to women.

Government incentives and programs such as the Arizona Registrar of Contractors (ROC) Women in Construction Program aim to increase the numbers of women working construction and running construction businesses. Unfortunately, there are still challenges facing women in construction. Many female construction workers feel they are not welcomed into the industry, and that the work environments can sometimes even be hostile. Much of the work is physically demanding, and many women are unable to handle the labor requirements.

Despite the obstacles, there are women who have enjoyed long, successful careers in the construction industry. Marlene O'Donnell, for example, is a sixty-five-year-old woman who co-owns a plastering firm in Santa Clara, California. "I've been in this business 32 years, and I have always been well treated," says Marlene. She has seen an increase in the number of project managers who are women. The number of women-owned construction firms is also on the rise, having increased by 35% from 1997 to 2002.

One of the biggest problems facing women in construction is that there are simply not many young women who consider construction as a career option. Arcadia Maximo, the owner of a small San Francisco-based construction firm, says, "Construction work was the last thing on my mind coming out of high school . . . it is just not something that is introduced to girls—that this is a viable career."

Electricians—another specialty trade—can look forward to an employment increase of 12 percent through 2008.

- *Glaziers* are responsible for selecting, cutting, installing, replacing, and removing all types of glass.

- *Insulation workers* line and cover structures with insulating materials.

- *Painters* and *paperhangers* stain, varnish, and apply other finishes to buildings and other structures and apply decorative coverings to walls and ceilings.

- *Pipelayers, plumbers, pipefitters,* and *steamfitters* install, maintain, and repair many different types of pipe systems. They may also install heating and cooling equipment and mechanical control systems.

- *Plasterers* and *stucco masons* apply plaster, concrete, stucco, and similar materials to interior and exterior walls and ceilings.

- *Roofers* repair and install roofs made of tar or asphalt and gravel; rubber or thermoplastic; metal; or shingles made of asphalt, slate, fiberglass, wood, tile, or other material.

- *Sheet metal workers* fabricate, assemble, install, and repair products and equipment made out of sheet metal, such as duct systems; roofs; siding; and drainpipes.

- *Structural* and *reinforcing iron* and *metal workers* place and install iron or steel girders, columns, and other structural members to form completed structures or frameworks of buildings, bridges, and other structures.

- *Construction laborers* perform a wide range of physically demanding tasks at building and highway construction sites, such as tunnel and shaft excavation, hazardous waste removal, environmental remediation, and demolition.

- *Helpers* assist trades workers and perform duties requiring less skill.

MANAGERS

Construction supervisors and managers oversee trades workers and helpers, and ensure that work is done well, safely, and according to code. They plan the job, resolve problems, and make sure work is completed on time. Those with the best organizational skills and supervisory ability may advance to higher construction management occupations, including project manager, field manager, or superintendent. These workers are responsible for getting a project completed on schedule by working with the *architect*'s plans, making sure materials are delivered on time, assigning work, overseeing supervisors, and ensuring that every phase of the project is completed quickly and properly.

CIVIL ENGINEERS

Civil engineers apply the principles of mathematics and physics to plan, design, and supervise the construction of roads, buildings, airports, tunnels, dams, bridges, and water supply and sewage systems. They must consider many factors in the design process, including construction costs, expected lifetime of a project, government regulations, environmental impact, and potential *natural disasters.* Civil engineering includes many sub-specialties, such as structural, water resources, construction, transportation, environmental and geotechnical engineering. Many civil engineers hold management or administrative positions, from supervisor of a construction site to city engineer.

Related Occupations in Construction

Other specialized non-construction trades also contribute work to construction projects:

• Architects design and draw plans for a building; many are also involved in supervising construction of the building.

• Elevator installers and repairers assemble, install, and replace elevators, escalators, moving walkways, and similar equipment in new and old buildings.

• Heating, air-conditioning, and refrigeration mechanics and installers install systems that control the temperature, humidity, and the total air quality in residential, commercial, industrial, and other buildings.

• Material moving occupations use machinery to move construction materials, earth, and other heavy materials, and clean vehicles, machinery, and other equipment.

• Assemblers and fabricators make and assemble products, ranging from toys to cars, as well as the parts that go into them.

• Highway maintenance workers maintain roads and highways.

What Will You Earn?

According to the Bureau of Labor Statistics, wages in construction are higher than the average for all industries. In 2008, production workers in construction averaged $21.87 an hour, or about $842 a week. In general, the jobs requiring more education and training, such as electricians and plumbers, get paid more than the trades requiring less education and training, such as laborers and helpers. (The boxed material at the end of each chapter in this book will also give you an idea as to what salaries you can expect for different types of construction jobs.)

Pay will also vary according to a worker's education, experience, type of work, complexity of the project, and geographic location. In addition, weather can affect the wages of construction workers, as workers are usually not paid when work has to stop for bad weather. Winter has often been a low period for construction work, especially in colder climates, but there is a trend toward more year-round construction.

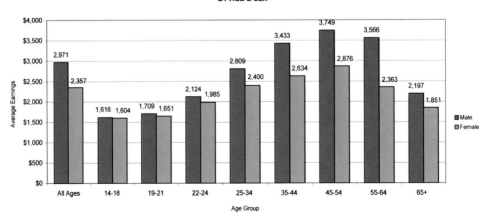

On average, men earn more than women in the construction industry.

If You Have an Enterprising Personality . . .

Here are some of the best jobs for you within the green construction industry.

JOB	ANNUAL EARNINGS	ANNUAL OPENINGS
construction managers	$76,230	44,158
first-line supervisors of construction trades	$55,950	82,923
engineering managers	$111,020	7,404

UNIONS

A union is an organization of workers that is formed to help protect the rights of all workers in that sector. Workers pay dues, or fees, to the union so that the union will bargain with the employer over issues such as wages, *benefits*, or improvement of work conditions.

About 17 percent of construction workers are union members or covered by union contracts. Union workers are usually paid more than nonunion workers and have better benefits. Many different unions represent the various construction trades and form committees with employers to supervise apprenticeship programs.

Don't follow trends—start trends.

—Frank Capra

ABOUT THE QUOTE

As you choose your career path for the future, no matter what direction you decide to go, you have the power to shape a new trend of respect for the Earth.

CHAPTER **5**
THE FUTURE OF CONSTRUCTION

WORDS TO KNOW

Baby Boomers: The generation of people born in the years following World War II, when there was an increase in birthrate.

Construction is one of the country's largest industries—it is also one of the industries predicted to need the most new workers in the coming years. The United States Bureau of Labor Statistics estimates that from 2006–2016, the construction industry will add 2,486,000 new jobs to the economy. Growth is expected to be fastest for jobs in nonresidential construction and special trades contractors in building and heavy construction.

Population growth, deteriorating infrastructure, and aging buildings will generate the new jobs in the construction industry. New green construction and green updates to existing buildings will add additional opportunities. Overall, job outlook is expected to be good for construction workers, especially those with the most experience and skill.

JOB OUTLOOK

RESIDENTIAL CONSTRUCTION

Residential construction is expected to grow moderately over the decade to meet the needs of a growing population. As the children of the *baby boomers* reach their peak house-buying years in the coming decade, demand for housing is expected to grow. In addition, an expanding older population will increase the need for senior housing and healthcare residences.

NONRESIDENTIAL CONSTRUCTION

Employment opportunities are also expected to increase in the nonresidential construction sector. Many industrial plants will have to be replaced or remodeled. The growing elderly population will increase the need for the construction of medical treatment facilities.

CIVIL ENGINEERING

Many of the country's highways, streets, and bridges are deteriorating. Employment in heavy and civil engineering construction is expected to increase as states and local governments approve budgets to replace or repair this crumbling infrastructure.

SPECIALTY TRADES

The largest number of new jobs is expected to be created in specialty trades contracting, because it is the largest segment of the industry. The number of jobs will grow as demand increases for subcontractors in new building and heavy construction, and as more workers are needed to repair and remodel existing homes,

Sort by Occupation Title (Sorted initially by Projected Need)	Sort by Projected Need for Employees (2006 - 2016)	Sort by Projected Growth	Sort by (Median) 2008 Hourly Wage Range[2]			Sort by (College degree) Education & Training[3]		
			Bottom 10%	Median	Top 10%	High School or less	Some College	College degree or higher
Environmental Science and Protection Technicians, Including Health — Description	State Report	24,000	27.%	$12	$19	$31	20%	37%	43%
Environmental Scientists and Specialists, Including Health — Description	State Report	42,000	18-26%	$17	$29	$49	1%	7%	92%
Environmental Engineers — Description	State Report	30,000	18-26%	$22	$36	$56	5%	9%	86%
Surveyors — Description	State Report	33,000	18-26%	$14	$25	$41	3%	22%	75%
Geoscientists, Except Hydrologists and Geographers — Description	State Report	15,000	18-26%	$20	$38	$75	1%	7%	92%
Industrial Engineers — Description	State Report	89,000	18-26%	$23	$35	$52	8%	24%	68%
Interior Designers — Description	State Report	33,000	18-26%	$13	$22	$40	16%	34%	50%
Technical Writers — Description	State Report	24,000	18-26%	$18	$30	$47	6%	20%	74%
Cost Estimators — Description	State Report	86,000	18-26%	$16	$27	$45	29%	41%	30%
Surveying and Mapping Technicians — Description	State Report	29,000	18-26%	$10	$17	$28	38%	55%	7%
Civil Engineers — Description	State Report	114,000	18-26%	$23	$36	$56	4%	12%	84%
Architects, Except Landscape and Naval — Description	State Report	48,000	18-26%	$20	$34	$57	2%	10%	86%
Construction and Building Inspectors — Description	State Report	40,000	18-26%	$15	$24	$38	30%	46%	24%

This table lists some of the jobs that are projected to grow the most in 2008, as well as the amount of education required to work in these fields.

which specialty trade contractors are more likely to perform. Carpenters and electricians top the list of specialty trades with the highest projected need for employees, at 348,000 and 234,000 respectively.

GREEN JOBS

Job outlook will be very good for construction workers with specialization in green building. Based on projected growth rates, the most in-demand construction workers will be those technicians specializing in environmental science and protection. In fact, four out of the top-five fastest-growing construction occupations are environmental in nature. Green construction is gaining importance rapidly!

Many of the new green jobs will be created in the heavy construction industry, including earth moving (crane operators, bulldozer operators), building roads, bridges, water infrastructure, power infrastructure, and government projects. Many green job opportunities will also be available in both the residential and nonresidential building sectors, as attempts are made to increase energy efficiency and reduce emissions.

> **Did You Know?**
> President Obama has proposed creating over 5 million new green construction jobs over the next decade!

WHO WILL GET THE JOBS?

Experienced workers, and those with a good work history or prior military service should enjoy the best job outlook. A variety of factors can affect competition for positions. Job prospects will be

Lifecycle Building Challenge

The Lifecycle Building Challenge is a national web-based competition sponsored by the EPA, the American Institute of Architects, West Coast Green, the Collaborative for High Performance Schools, and StopWaste.org. The challenge "invites professionals and students to submit ideas for buildings and products that are created for adaptation, disassembly, or dismantling for recovery." This means that the buildings are designed with deconstruction in mind, so that the buildings can be reused in future buildings.

Here are some of the ideas from Lifecycle Building Challenge entrants:

- A recreational building that breaks into 3 parts for transportation by truck to a new site.
- The green mobile home with detachable rooms allowing for additions or remodeling.
- A plug-in home with a specialized connector joint, allowing components to be unplugged quickly and without damage.
- Zip tape that allows drywall to be easily removed and reused.

The Arboretum and Research Visitor's Center in Charlottesville, Virginia, was the 2009 winner for Professional Building and won an outstanding achievement award for Best Greenhouse Gas Reduction.

best for workers willing and able to get the needed certifications, licenses, training, and education required for specialized occupations, such as crane operators, electricians, plumbers, pipefitters, and steamfitters. On the opposite end, jobs that require no specialized skill or training will have the worst job outlook.

Other jobs that will have lower competition and therefore a more positive outlook are those jobs that are dangerous, physically demanding, or expose workers to extreme conditions. Roofers, for example, are expected to have good job prospects, because of industry growth combined with difficult working conditions. Workers willing to face these risks or rigorous demands will have better job prospects.

In all cases, a familiarity with green construction requirements—or better yet official certification from GBCI, LEED, or another green certification program—will give a worker an advantage over other job applicants.

If You Have a Conventional Personality . . .

Here are some of the best jobs for you within the green construction industry.

JOB	ANNUAL EARNINGS	ANNUAL OPENINGS
inspectors, testers, sorters, samplers, & weighers	$30,310	75,361

FURTHER READING

Byers, Ann. *Jobs As Green Builders and Planners* (Green Careers). New York: Rosen Publishing, 2010.

Deitche, Scott M. *Green Collar Jobs: Environmental Careers for the 21st Century*. Santa Barbara, Calif.: Praeger, 2010.

Fehl, Pamela. *Business and Construction* (Green Careers). New York: Ferguson, 2010.

Mondschein, Kenneth C. *Construction and Trades* (Great Careers with a High School Diploma). New York: Ferguson, 2005.

Sumichrast, Michael. *Opportunities in Building Construction Careers*. New York: McGraw-Hill, 2008.

FIND OUT MORE ON THE INTERNET

Associated Builders and Contractors
www.trytools.org

Career Compass
www.careervoyages.gov/careercompass-main.cfm

Green Mechanical Council
www.greenmech.org

Home Builder's Institute
www.hbi.org

National Association of Home Builders
www.nahb.org

National Center for Construction Education and Research
www.nccer.org

State Apprenticeship Programs
www.doleta.gov/oa

DISCLAIMER

The websites listed on this page were active at the time of publication. The publisher is not responsible for websites that have changed their address or discontinued operation since the date of publication. The publisher will review and update the websites upon each reprint.

BIBLIOGRAPHY

California Department of Industrial Relations, "I Built It," www.dir.ca.gov/DAS/IBuiltIt/youth-what-you-can-do.html (8 February 2010).

Career Voyages, "Where Will the Demands Be," www.careervoyages.gov/students-main.cf. (10 February 2010).

The Center of Construction Research and Training (CPWR). *The Construction Chart Book: The U.S. Construction Industry and Its Workers*, fourth edition. Silver Spring, Ma.: CPWR, 2007.

DBEnterprises. "Women Build Ranks." *DBE/EEO Opportunities on the Hiawatha Light Rail Project*, Issue 11, 2003.

Revkin, Andrew C. "Global Warming." *The New York Times*, December 8, 2009. http://topics.nytimes.com/top/news/science/topics/globalwarming/index.html (5 February 2010).

United States Bureau of Labor Statistics. *Issues in Labor Statistics: Current Trends in Construction Employment*. Washington, D.C.: U.S. Department of Labor, 2007.

_____. *Women in the Labor Force: A Databook*. Washington, D.C.: U.S. Department of Labor, 2008.

United States Department of Labor, Bureau of Labor Statistics, "Construction," www.bls.gov/oco/ocos248.htm (4 February 2010).

United States Environmental Protection Agency, "Climate Change," www.epa.gov/climatechange/basicinfo.html (5 February 2010).

United States Environmental Protection Agency, "Green Building," www.epa.gov/greenbuilding/ (5 February 2010).

INDEX

About the Author

Malinda Miller lives and works in upstate New York. After earning a graduate degree in anthropology, she found work at a small publisher, where she enjoys the opportunity to research and write on a variety of topics.

About the Consultant

Michael Puglisi is the director of the Department of Labor's Workforce New York One Stop Center in Binghamton, New York. He has also held several leadership positions in the International Association of Workforce Professionals (IAWP), a non-profit educational association exclusively dedicated to workforce professionals with a rich tradition and history of contributions to workforce excellence. IAWP members receive the tools and resources they need to effectively contribute to the workforce development system daily. By providing relevant education, timely and informative communication and valuable findings of pertinent research, IAWP equips its members with knowledge, information and practical tools for success. Through its network of local and regional chapters, IAWP is preparing its members for the challenges of tomorrow.

Picture Credits

Fotolia.com:
    AndreasG pp. 1, 3, 5, 8, 18, 28, 40, 54
    Andres Rodriguez p. 54
    Djoxy p. 40

Thomas Perkins p. 15
Stephen Coburn p. 12
Domen Colja p. 18
Lisa F. Young pp. 28, 34, 48
Ernest Prim p. 44
Yahia LOUKKAL p. 8

To the best knowledge of the publisher, all images not specifically credited are in the public domain. If any image has been inadvertently uncredited, please notify Harding House Publishing Service, 220 Front Street, Vestal, New York 13850, so that credit can be given in future printings.